LOST C...
AFRICA'S KINGDOM OF PLEASURE

• LOST CITY •

A ROYAL WELCOME

'In Xanadu did Kubla Khan a stately pleasure dome decree...' When Samuel Taylor Coleridge penned his vision in a dream two hundred years ago, he could just as easily have been describing the Lost City and its splendid Palace. A two-hour drive from Johannesburg across the dusty Highveld, with its hillside explosions of fiery aloes and its waving grasses shimmering under the sun as far as the eye can see, brings the visitor to the awesome spectacle that is The Palace of the Lost City *(left)*.

• SEAT OF KINGS •

Leaving the flat plains behind and weaving between the gentle hills that rim the extinct volcano of the Pilanesberg, visitors are swept over a low bridge *(above)* while their senses are treated to an effusion of spectacularly unexpected sights and sounds.

The Cheetah Fountain *(right)*, silhouetted against the entrance, draws visitors into the magical, surreal world of the Lost City. Sable heads in the porte-cochere *(opposite, top right)* echo the many vaults and arches of the hotel in the eloquently grand arcs of their horns, and serve as a fittingly majestic welcome to this watery wonderland.

3

• LOST CITY •

CARVED OUT OF AFRICA

The Lost City is a bewitching trompe l'oeil of the 'old' and the new. Although it was built from scratch, an enchanting depth has been lent to the fantasy by bestowing on it a regal 'history' stretching back into the mists of time.

The 'legend' of the Lost City tells of a wandering tribe that found a secluded valley in which it built a civilisation of peace and plenty. The heart of the settlement was The Palace, an architectural monument worthy of the people's benevolent king. An earthquake, the story goes, destroyed the community and its buildings, and the ruins lay mouldering under creeping vegetation until 1991, when they were 'rediscovered' and 'restored' to their former glory.

FANTASY FAÇADES

Mirrored by the still waters of crystal-clear pools and flanked by the bubbling effervescence of rivers, streams and waterfalls, The Palace today sits in august grandeur on a hill looking upon the Valley of the Ancients. Unmistakably African in the age-stressed, rose-coloured, concrete walls, there are also hints of India in the graceful domes, spicy tastes of Turkey in the delicate minarets, and whispers of Vienna in the polished marble expanses.

• LOST CITY •

OF CRYSTALS AND KINGS

The light-filled, mosaic-and-fresco entrance rotunda of The Palace *(above)* draws visitors ever deeper into the mythical world of the Lost City; even the lofty potted palms are dwarfed by the cathedral-like immensity of its scale. The crowning glory is the jungle-fantasy painted dome *(left)*, 25 metres above, which tells, in six immaculate, Renaissance-style panels, of baobabs and baboons, predators and prey, in a land that time forgot. The rich glow of the hand-laid mosaic floor emanates from 300 000 pieces of marble and granite in 38 shades.

• ROYAL ENTRANCE AND CRYSTAL COURT •

A stroll across the hand-polished floor of the Royal Entrance Chamber takes visitors onto a landing overlooking the breathtaking Crystal Court *(above)*, a grand salon that offers both fine dining and relaxed cocktails to the accompaniment of Bach and Beethoven. A sweeping marble staircase *(above left)* edged with a balustrade of rock crystal and bronze guides the eye to the centrepiece of the Crystal Court, an imposing fountain held aloft by four trumpeting denizens of the plains *(left)*. Their backward-curling trunks playfully spray water into a huge bronze bowl and echo one of the most fittingly majestic themes of The Palace: that of the elephant, age-old, dignified, deeply African.

• LOST CITY •

TUSKERS AND TORTOISES

The glass-roofed Elephant Walk *(above left)* leads to a sun-drenched courtyard in which a monument to Shawu, one of the Kruger Park's 'magnificent seven' bull elephants who were renowned for the size of their tusks, stands alone, frozen in time, the aggressive turn of his head above his huge bronze tusks never to be completed *(above and left)*.

The immensity of the scale of the Lost City and its Palace is charmingly counterpoised by representations of the smaller creatures of the wild. Around the Grand Pool *(opposite, top)*, overlooked by the five domed pavilions of the Villa del Palazzo restaurant, stone turtles lift their ancient heads to the sun and crocodiles bask

• ELEPHANT WALK AND GRAND POOL •

in the summer heat. The clear waters of the Grand Pool are fed by a huge clam shell out of which water cascades in a continuous flow. The brilliant mosaic in the depths of the pool tell the story of another 'legend' of the Lost City, the two huge, blue suns on either side of the pool representative of the warring stars Los and Nus. Four pavilions, one at each corner of the pool area, provide drinks, light meals and suntanning paraphernalia. Poolside palm trees echo the tropical theme of the gardens below, while a nearby hillside of baobabs remind guests that this is Africa.

• LOST CITY •

SUMPTUOUS SUNDOWNERS

The regal opulence of The Palace is perhaps best experienced in the evenings, when leaping flames and electric light turn its fluid surrounds into a shimmering wonderland. Guests have a number of options to choose from, and may begin their evening in the Crystal Court where they can watch the sun set through the seven-metre-high, arched windows *(left)*, while being gently serenaded by grand piano or strings.

• EVENING SERENADE •

On the marble landing overlooking the glittering Crystal Court *(opposite, right)*, a string quartet gives a special performance before an evening audience.

Sunsets lend an orange-hued aura to the Valley of the Ancients. If the weather is balmy, guests may relax on the sweeping verandah of the Crystal Court, overlooking the Valley of the Waves *(above right)*. The Villa del Palazzo *(right)*, another jungle fantasy complete with painted cupola ceiling, hand-carved chairs representing various wild animals and clerestory windows overlooking the Grand Pool, is a luxurious dinner option, turning fine dining into an art with its regional Italian cuisine.

• LOST CITY •

VERDANT VISIONS

'And there were gardens bright with sinuous rills, where blossomed many an incense-bearing tree; and here were forests ancient as the hills, enfolding sunny spots of greenery.' Imagination and fantasy have carved out of the parched savanna a 25-hectare jungle of dream proportions. Soft mist plays in the rainforests, droplets of water gleaming like jewels on the orchids that hang from the branches; tropical ebony, milkwood and flame trees whisper their African heritage while birds both indigenous and exotic, such as the macaw *(opposite, below left),* call from

• JUNGLE PARADISE •

the canopy; hillsides of transplanted baobab trees look as if they have been there from the beginning of time. And everywhere, running water in a myriad forms – tinkling streams, cascading falls, rushing rivers – soothes and enchants.

The swing bridge *(right)*, spanning a river between tangles of forest, invites the surefooted to walk its rope-and-wood length. The Gong of the Sun Lion *(above)*, magnificently lit up at night and overlooking both the amphitheatre and the Royal Baths, is occasionally sounded to herald the announcement of events of import in times past.

• LOST CITY •

STAIRWAY TO THE STARS

'... *holy and enchanted...*' The Royal Staircase *(above right)*, once the exclusive passageway of kings and princes, today allows guests of more common descent to follow in the footsteps of royalty. From the imposing East Gate of The Palace, the steep staircase descends, intersected by bubbling streams of water in which dancing flames reflect at night, to the Royal Baths *(opposite)*. Time-stressed rock carved with

ROYAL ARENA AND BATHS

mythical symbols surround the still waters of the Baths; the nearby ancient Observatory *(opposite, below right)* carries through the theme, incised with a star chart said to have been used by seers of old. Here, visitors will be reminded of the dual-sun mosaic that lies in the depths of the Grand Pool, a hint as to the importance played by celestial bodies in the lives of the ancients. The Observatory today serves a more prosaic function, however: that of refreshment centre to guests, who can sip cocktails while watching the surf roll down the Valley of Waves.

• LOST CITY •

WATER WONDERLAND

'*Five miles meandering with a mazy motion through wood and dale the sacred river ran...*' Twenty three million litres of water circulate through the grounds of The Palace, rushing around its buildings, cascading down its rock faces, swirling into its pools and winding through its forests. Gem of this water wonderland is the Valley of Waves *(above and left)* with its Caribbean-style, blue bay and its traceries of quiet waterways on which guests can ride on inflatable tubes. Throughout the Valley there

• VALLEY OF WAVES •

are water features wherever you look, including 13 major waterfalls, 20 cascades, two mountain rivers and six wetland areas.

The Wave Pool *(above and right)* laps onto a blinding white beach of crushed stone from nearby mines, over which sway palm trees that echo the soaring spires of The Palace on the skyline. While their parents relax on the beach, children can play safely in the Crocodile Cove or the Hippo Haven and scramble to their hearts' content about the Rickety Rock.

• LOST CITY •

SUN AND SURF

The scallop-shaped Wave Pool *(above and right)* was once the village swimming pool, or so the story goes. The mythical earthquake that ravaged the ancient city and its surrounds is said to have released a giant underground geyser which today periodically pushes to the surface to create swells perfect for both body and board surfing. So real are the waves that surge from the base of the rock wall that the Wave Pool has played host to

18

• VALLEY OF WAVES •

national surfing championships *(right)* and is rated by those in the know to provide better surf than 50 percent of South Africa's coastal locales! The surf is an ideal height (up to 1,86 metres) and the impressive line of waves runs for a useful distance of over 30 metres.

Overlooked by the regal towers of The Palace, holidaymakers far from the sea can sport dolphin-like in the cool waters of the Wave Pool, wander the expanses of beach, sip cooldrinks at any of the 'seaside' refreshment centres, or doze the afternoon away under thatched umbrellas *(above)*. Like everywhere at the Lost City, adventure is there for the taking ... but idleness is also acceptable!

• LOST CITY •

TAKING THE PLUNGE

The Valley of Waves caters for all tastes, and for the most adventurous, there is the heart-stopping waterslide, including a 97-metre drop, which starts high above the Valley in the aptly named Temple of Courage *(above)*. With a breathtaking view of the waterworld from the top, the ride catapults revellers down an almost-vertical drop *(left and opposite, above right)*, sending them underground for a spine-chilling few seconds before depositing them in a spray

• VALLEY OF WAVES •

of water in the pool at the bottom. The most pulse-quickening event that might befall a cooldrink-sipping sailor on the 500-metre Lazy River Ride *(right)* is receiving a cooling spray of water from a stone elephant's trunk. Inflatable tubes are the mode of transport on this ride, bobbing gently down the stream that encircles an alfresco refreshment area. Safe, shallow pools provide hours of entertainment for children *(above)*.

21

• LOST CITY •

SPANNING THE AGES

'*And from this chasm, with ceaseless turmoil seething...*' Modern holidaymakers who cross the Bridge of Time *(above)* under the watchful gaze of an elephant guard of honour, passing beneath the gimlet gaze of the leopard guardian of the Temple of Creation *(left)*, are reminded of the massive earthquake that destroyed the original city by the periodic explosions of smoke and steam that emanate from the Temple, causing

• BRIDGE OF TIME •

the Bridge to tremble and shake. The Bridge ties ancient history to modern-day fun, a stately passageway between the time-worn magnificence of The Palace and its grounds, and the new-age Entertainment Centre. With its animal theme dominated by monkeys, the Bridge is flanked on The Palace side by the ten-metre-high Mighty Kong Gates *(above right)* and the Sacred Monkey Plaza, central focus of which is the Monkey Spring Fountain *(above left)*, an elemental creation of stone, water and fire.

• LOST CITY •

ROMANCE AND REFLECTIONS

'*The shadow of the dome of pleasure floated midway on the waves...*'
The Palace, a luxurious retreat from everyday realities, seems suspended in its watery environs, and the reflections of its myriad lights play sparkling games with its rivers and pools. Beyond the perimeters of the Lost City, in the Pilanesberg National Park, the daytime animals are finding refuge for the night while those that hunt under the moon are abroad on velvet paws and whispering wings. Within the landscaped gardens, the stone animals that brave the heat of the day, by night stand in majestic silence under the soft glow of a thousand lights.

• AFTER DARK •

Inside, meanwhile, all is sound and light. Swimming, tennis and golf give way to more leisurely pastimes as The Palace's numerous bars and entertainment areas start business for the evening; cocktail dresses take the place of bathing costumes and muted music wafts through the vaulted passageways of the hotel. Pre-dinner drinks give way to leisurely meals as guests prepare to explore the delights of the Lost City by night.

25

• LOST CITY •

SUPER SLOTS

The Entertainment Centre, with its fibre-optically created Milky Way ceiling and cascading chandelier *(above left)*, draws guests into another fantasy world, one in which night-time is the right time. Banks of slot machines preside in the Hall of Treasures, and the Dream Machine lures punters with the possibility of a fortune at the flick of a button. The jungle theme is carried through in opulent fashion, the centrepiece of three lofty giraffes with necks entwined looks down benignly on the revellers far below *(above right)*.

• ENTERTAINMENT •

EXTRAVAGANT ENTERTAINMENT

Birds of paradise in human form lend brilliance to evening entertainment *(above left and right)*, in extravaganzas showcasing the best and the brightest in international entertainment. For productions on an awe-inspiring scale there is the 6 000-seater Superbowl *(above right)*, across whose glittering stage have danced the likes of Queen, Rod Stewart and Liza Minnelli, and which has hosted Miss World pageants, world-title boxing and other major sporting events.

• LOST CITY •

THE SPIN OF THE WHEEL

For more serious gamblers, a fortune may lie on the turn of a card. In the celebrated Casino *(above)* in The Sun City Hotel, punters play blackjack and roulette, and in between games ease out in front of the slot machines. Another gambling venue is the Entertainment Centre. Under the gleaming curves of a pair of elephants with jewel-encrusted tusks, more modest gamesmen may try their luck at slot machines with lower stakes *(opposite, above left)*,

• ENTERTAINMENT •

and participation video games *(above right)* offer youngsters the opportunity to flip a Formula-One racing car around a track or travel into outer space to do battle with aliens.

Lavish formal dinners held under the auspices of the large conference centre allow guests the opportunity of further exploring the Entertainment Centre, mixing business with pleasure in a delightfully luxurious setting *(right)*.

29

• LOST CITY •

DESERT DRIVES

'Sublime to look at and exciting to play' is the way Gary Player planned the 55-hectare, 18-hole, 72-par, desert-style golf course on the perimeters of the Lost City – and that is exactly what it is. The Gary Player Design Company's uncomplicated use of the undulating landscape lends quirky complexity to the course, each hole of which has a minimum of three tee positions, most on different levels. From everywhere on the course there are magnificent views of The Palace and its surrounds.

30

• LOST CITY GOLF COURSE •

In line with the Lost City's magically African theme, crocodiles patrol the depths of the water hazard in front of the 13th hole *(right)*, and different tones of sand colour are used in the bunkers. The club house *(opposite, top)* and its lavish interior *(opposite, below left)* fit similarly into the theme, apparently housed in one of the ruins of the Lost City, its tumbles of honey-coloured stones mellowing under the Highveld sun.

• LOST CITY •

PALACE OF PLEASURE

'... *a miracle of rare device...*' Until a few short years ago, the lovely valley of the Pilanesberg nursed a secret: under the tumbles of rocks and creeping vegetation, the foundations of an ancient civilisation lay sleeping in the midday sun. Today, the Lost City combines the splendour of that mythical age with every modern comfort, to create a futuristic fun palace that draws millions of tourists every year. No hotel built to resemble a palace, but rather a palace that serves as a hotel, the Lost City is carved from the heart of old Africa, but is very much part of the new. The Palace awaits ... to bewitch, to pamper, to welcome you into a world like no other.